Lost sheep found: A Social History Of The Muggletonians.

By William Hatfield

Acknowledgements

First and foremost, I would like to thank my dissertation supervisor, Tim Reinke-Williams, for all the support and feedback. I would like to thank my peers and friends for helping to put this together and for highlighting my many, many mistakes. I would like to thank my family and partner for keeping my morale up. Finally, I would like to thank Lodowick Muggleton and John Reeve for providing me with such an interesting topic to research.

Introduction.

'I have chosen thee, my last messenger, for a great work, unto this bloody unbelieving world; and I have given thee Lodowick Muggleton to be thy mouth.'[1]

In writing these words, John Reeve established one of the most unique religious sects in the history of the English revolution. This group grew around the nucleus of a revelation that John Reeve believed he received from Jesus Christ himself. In this, Reeve

---

[1] John Reeve and Lodowick Muggleton 'A Transcendent Spiritual Treatises' in in *The Acts of the Witnesses : The Autobiography of Lodowick Muggleton and Other Early Muggletonian Writings*, ed. by T. L. Underwood, (Oxford University Press, Incorporated, 2000.) p.142.

believed that Christ gave him an ability to understand scripture like the Lord himself. He was told his cousin, Lodowick Muggleton was to join him in spreading the word of his revelation and that the antichrist was his former associate and radical Ranter, John Robins. Thus, with this, the Muggletonians were born. Rising out of their community in central London to form sects as far as Ireland[2], this group has often been overlooked and overshadowed by its more 'exciting' counterparts such as the Diggers, Ranters and Levellers. However, when cracking open the mild shell of the Muggletonians, a unique, complex and often overlooked social history emerges. This work

---
[2] F. D. Dow . *Radicalism in the English Revolution 1640-1660*. (Oxford: Blackwell, 1985.) p.69

will focus on the history of their views regarding gender, their community life and how they fit into their generation. It aims to expand it in order to provide a more in-depth and well-rounded social historiography of the Muggletonians.

Understanding this current historiography of the Muggletonians can aid in explaining why the social history of the Muggletonians is often left unnoticed. When studying the Muggletonians, historians have often gone one of two paths, either the history from below, the more Marxist view of Christopher Hill or a simple explanation of such a minor group with little opinion outside the idea that their beliefs were vaguely disconcerting. Andrew

Bradstock highlights this when discussing his reasons for studying the Muggletonians, stating that despite their comparatively large size and longevity, they have been largely forgotten due to their views.[3] This seems to be a consensus, that the rather mild views of the Muggletonians lead to both their survival for 300 years but also continued ignorance of them since. This is shown best by Ronald Hutton who remarks, 'These "Muggletonians" aroused little interest in the country at large because they were both cautious and quietist.', Hutton himself seems to prove this theory, with less than half a page in his book

---

[3] Andrew Bradstock. *Radical Religion in Cromwell's England : A Concise History from the English Civil War to the End of the Commonwealth,* (I. B. Tauris & Company, Limited, 2010.) p. 139.

dedicated to the group, using them as a mere transition to the smaller, yet far more tantalising group of the Diggers. [4]

The more Marxist approach that Hill presented also seems to have permeated into the historiography of the Muggletonians. F.D. Dow remarks and expands on Hill's work by discussing the wealth and work of those that the Muggletonians attracted. Dow references Hill's discussion of their comparatively higher wealth while adding his own insights into the actual work that they partook in, discussing them as merchants, shopkeepers, and artisans. Dow goes further by adding that the group was

---

[4] Ronald Hutton, *The British Republic 1649-1660*. (2nd ed. Basingstoke: Macmillan, 2000.) P.31.

decisively unattractive to the average labourer or servant and that the main bulk of Muggletonian support came from the literate middling orders.[5] This over-prevalence and over-reliance on Hill and the Marxist viewpoint often problematically leaves the Muggletonians being seen as a group of eccentric, well off gentlemen, disconnected from the social climate of their day. However, coming out of the bustling workers' hub of London, this conclusion is problematic at best.

While the Muggletonians themselves may not have formed distinct and separate communities like the Diggers at St George's Hill, strong communal

---

[5] Dow, *Radicalism in the English Revolution 1640-1660*. p.68.

bonds did develop within the believers as Juleen Audrey Eichinger highlights in her dissertation work.[6] Eichinger highlights that the Muggletonian community grew around a system of events and meetings as opposed to a strong physical outwards presence like the Ranters. This is supported by R. C. Richardson who describes them as an 'informal, self-effacing organization.'.[7] Yet neither of these historians explains how communal bonds enabled the movement to form and grow. This is a glaring hole in the historiography of the Muggletonians. In truth, the organization seems to have grown out of John Reeve's local community in the heart of

---

[6] Juleen Audrey Eichinger, The Muggletonians: A People Apart (Dissertation: West Michigan University, 1999) pp.196-197.
[7] R.C. Richardson, The Debate on the English Revolution (Manchester: Manchester University Press, 1998) p.198.

working-class London, the primary example of this being that in *A Transcendent Spiritual Treatise*, the individuals that 'Jesus' tells Reeve to collect are all people from his family, community or former social circles. This extended to other members of the Muggletonians too.

Lawrence Clarkson writes in his work, *The lost sheep found* about concern for his local parish surrounding a ministerial order regarding guidelines on the receiving of the sacrament.[8] It is clear that at least at some level, community and care for that community play a role in influencing the mindsets of many Muggletonians. While the

---

[8] Lawrence Clarkson, The Lost Sheep Found, (London: Printed for the author, 1660) p.4.

infighting within the Muggletonian leadership that Christopher Hill has highlighted may have been perceived as an issue, the sense of Muggletonian community that was garnered outweighed any infighting as meetings continued to be held and unified notes were held for the next 300 years. [9]

This work adds to the historiography by examining the community life of the Muggletonians within their practices. It aims to establish just how truly important community was to the Muggletonians and whether this was the driving force for the group's actions and longevity. The Muggletonians also relied heavily on print. As Joad Raymond

---

[9] Christopher Hill. "The Muggletonians." *Past & Present*, no. 104 (1984) pp.154-156

highlights, the historiography of print in revolutionary England was initially ignored, bar the bright spot of Christopher Hill's work, and the Muggletonians seem to have been enveloped in this academic shadow. Yet as Raymond demonstrates, print networks had a huge effect from the top downwards on all aspects of social and communal life.[10] Muggletonian sources from the group's seventeenth-century membership, including Muggleton and Reeves' works, letters from several followers including Elizabeth Dickinson as well as poetry, songs and even a dinner itinerary will be

---

[10] Joad Raymond. *Seventeenth-Century Print Culture* (university of east Anglia, 2004) p.4.
<https://warwick.ac.uk/fac/arts/ren/researchcurrent/archive/newberry/collaborativeprogramme/ren-earlymod-communities/britishandamericanhistories/summerworkshop/knights/raymond_on_print.pdf>
[Last accessed 17/03/2022]

examined to help create a far more rounded picture of the Muggletonians as a community-driven unit.

One of the more historically neglected areas of study regarding the Muggletonians is looking at the role of gender within the Muggletonian cause. The most that Hill weighs in on this is regarding the views of a former Ranter turned Muggletonian, Lawrence Clarkson, reflecting on his previous views regarding sexuality. In this, he rejects his former views of sexual proclivity and instead favours a far more conservative view of sexual prudence. More interesting, however, Clarkson also seems to reject an arguably objectifying Ranter view of seeing all women as one with regards to sexual activity.[11] This idea that Hill fortuitously included from Clarkson seems to be emblematic of a larger trend of heavily supported female agency through the church. Keith Thomas highlighted this in his 1958 article where he uses the example of Jane Adams being reminded at church that her husband comes after her religious responsibilities.[12] Right from the outset of Reeve's vision, there seems to be something different regarding the Muggletonian's view of the role of women within their sect. When Reeve first received his revelation, the taking of a woman with him to meet Muggleton

---

[11] Christopher Hill, *The world turned upside down: Radical Ideas during the English Revolution.* (Penguin Books, 2019 edition.) p.241.
[12] Keith Thomas, "Women And The Civil War Sects", *Past & Present*, (Volume 13, Issue 1, April 1958) p.52.

was a key part of the vision given to him by 'Christ'.[13] This inclusion of women alongside men as equal role holders of the Muggletonian ideas is a key aspect of the Muggletonian belief system and one that is prevalent throughout the early writings of both Reeve and Muggleton. It is these writings that will provide much of the skeleton for looking at the social history of the Muggletonian cause. These documents are rich in the Muggletonian insights of every aspect of society imaginable.

Muggleton's writing on *A True Interpretation Of The Witch of Endor* reveals much of his insight towards women and, most interestingly, his rather progressive views on abortion. On the other hand,

---

[13] Reeve and Lodowick Muggleton, 'A Transcendent Spiritual Treatise.' p.143.

documents such as *A Looking Glass for George Fox* reveal not only Muggleton's views regarding the Quakers as a whole but his strong views on masculinity and the relationship between men and women. The role of women and masculinity in the English revolution is a well-documented one. Ann Hughes has examined the roles of women in radical movements such as the Quakers for example who had members such as Richard Farnworth who publicly proclaimed for the rights of women preachers yet private correspondence shows a degree of "Male alarm".[14] Similarly, Phyllis Mack highlights that female conversion to Quakerism was not a liberation, but rather repression, moving

---

[14]Ann Hughes, *Gender and the English Revolution*. (London: Routledge, 2012) p.84.

more into a group focussed mindset.[15] Ann Hughes also comments on the radical masculinities of men at the time, highlighting individuals such as Winstanley and Lilburne as key figures who used their masculinity in their radicalism.[16] However, this sort of in-depth view on both women and their roles as well as the roles of men and the influence of their masculinity does not appear to be prevalent in the study of the Muggletonians. This work will aim to rectify this by looking at the early works of the Muggletonians and assessing their attitudes towards women and their roles in the group as a whole as well as assessing what Reeves, Muggleton

---

[15] Phyllis Mack, *Visionary Women Ecstatic Prophecy in Seventeenth- Century England.* (London, University of California press, 1992) p.149.
[16] Ann Hughes, *Gender and the English Revolution.* pp.106-107.

and other primary Muggletonians viewed men's roles and the roles of masculinity in their movement to be.

Reeve and Muggleton's work, 'Joyful News From Heaven' reveals the pair's views of their generation and the radicalism therein. Alexandra Walsham weighs in on this generational radicalism, suggesting that this religious diversion and extremism was a result of a generation that saw the rebelling against a protestant orthodoxy as a necessary part of their religious experience. Walsham also suggests that the sectarianism that we see in the mid-seventeenth century is a result of institutionalised reform and the view of breaking with tradition and finding one's personal "inner light", as Walsham phrases it, is a standardized part of the lives of many in this generation.[17] The Muggletonians were clearly unable to escape this generation's gravitational pull towards sectarianism, yet their views when looking at other groups such as their contemporary rival, the Quakers, reveal an interesting view of themselves as the exception to the radical rule of the time. When looking at the generational views of the radical sects of England, one issue becomes increasingly pervasive and divisive, that of

---

[17] Alexandra Walsham, "The Reformation Of The Generations: Youth, Age And Religious Change In England, c. 1500–1700." *Transactions of the Royal Historical Society*, (vol. 21, 2011) p.114.

predestination. The Muggletonians fell on the side of accepting a Calvinist view of the topic. Christopher Hill highlights that Muggleton's own words surrounding the topic of predestination, provide a view of a man who was not enthused with the idea of heaven as it was traditionally shown, but rather fearful of hell. Muggleton himself seems to have preferred the view of 'soul sleeping', with Hill remarking that Muggleton may have preferred this to the more 'boring' view of heaven at the time.[18] These views may have been influenced by his partner John Reeve. Eichinger remarks upon Reeve's unique life as a religious nomad, travelling around various religious groups

---

[18] Christopher Hill, *The world turned upside down: Radical Ideas during the English Revolution*. pp.128-129.

including the Puritans, Ranters, and an affiliation with the extremely radical Ranter John Robins, whom he would later write about with regards to his 'visions', and finally a brief flirtation with Quakerism before receiving his 'visions'.[19] This idea of Reeve as a generational paradigm of radicalism may reveal why much of the early Muggletonian writings are so unique, even in a generation of radicals. Reeve, in this way, is very similar to Hill's prime example of Lawrence Clarkson, who also ended life as a Muggletonian when converted by Reeve.[20]

---

[19] Juleen Audrey Eichinger, "The Muggletonians: A People Apart" pp.129-130.
[20] Christopher Hill, *The world turned upside down: Radical Ideas during the English Revolution.* pp.160-162.

This attraction of seasoned radical sectarians would suggest the Muggletonians as a form of a culmination of a generation of radical sects for those in their middle age, a moderate endpoint for many after a misspent youth of more extreme radicalism. Eichinger seems to corroborate this idea in the conclusion of her dissertation, in which she highlights the many influences of Muggletonians, from strict Calvinism and the other seventeenth-century sects to "medial Joachism".[21] A generational view of the radical sects of the English revolution is ground that relatively few historians have tread upon. This work will attempt to address this glaring gap in the historiography by assessing

---

[21] Juleen Audrey Eichinger, "The Muggletonians: A People Apart" p.198.

the ways that the generation they belonged to influenced the Muggletonians. This will be done by looking at the primary works of the Muggletonians as well as their views and interactions with regard to the other radical sects that grew out of their generation to create a fuller picture of how generational differences affected the ways in which the Muggletonians formed and behaved.

Overall, this work will be split into 3 main chapters looking at the social history of the Muggletonians. The first will focus on the ways that the community surrounded, bonded and influenced the growth of the group. The next will focus on the roles of gender and masculinity within the group and what role it played in a group formed by, focussed upon and largely run by men and how deeply their unique views regarding women and women's rights penetrated their religious beliefs. The final chapter will look at the role that generational differences played in the group. It will look at the world that Muggletonianism formed in and those that influenced the founders and creators of the sect and will evaluate the generational foundation that the Muggletonians stood upon and the impact that it had on them.

Chapter 1: The Mugletonians' attitude towards women.

When thinking of radical religion in the 17th century, the word 'feminism' does not come to mind. Yet the Muggletonians had a rather unique worldview when it comes to their treatment and representation of women in their written works. The most evident way that this is shown is through the language and ideas that Muggleton wrote with when discussing the institution of marriage and his view of women within that. In what amounts to the biography of his religious life, *The acts of the Witnesses*, he recounts the story of himself finding a wife. One of the most illuminating details comes at the start of this tale when discussing the mother of his potential bride's decision to give her away. In response to this act of giving away her only daughter, he remarks that he feels 'Too inferiour for her'.[22] While this could be seen as a remark regarding his class status, yet the fact that Muggleton discusses his class in the prior paragraph and uses this one to focus on his worthiness with regards to her mother dispels this.[23]

His story continues with the recounting of not accepting this wife as she did not share his religious views. Yet, throughout all this, he never

---

[22] Lodowick Muggleton 'The acts of the Witnesses' in *The Acts of the Witnesses : The Autobiography of Lodowick Muggleton and Other Early Muggletonian Writings*, ed. by T. L. Underwood, (Oxford University Press, Oxford, 2000.) p.33.
[23] Muggleton 'The acts of the Witnesses' p.33.

once disparages this woman or her mother, in fact insulting her father as being 'hare-brained'. While the notion of female equality is not wholly unique to the world of radical English sects, with George Fox of the Quakers declared 'every man and woman, that be heirs of the gospel, are heirs of this authority.' alongside the rise of Quaker meetings established by and for women.[24] Where Muggleton seems to go further is his repeated alluding to gender egalitarianism within his sect. However, it is impossible to remove Muggleton from the context of his time and this is no more apparent than when viewing the discussions of his marriages.

---

[24] H. Larry Ingle. "A Quaker Woman on Women's Roles: Mary Penington to Friends, 1678." *Signs*, vol. 16, no. 3, (1991) p.589.

When reading Muggleton's descriptions of his wives, one aspect stands out, his repeated highlighting of the fact that these women, always his junior, are virgins. Virginity was expected in a wife to be throughout the medieval period and as Alice Brabcová points out, this tradition continued into the 17th century.[25] Although, as she points out, around 25% of women were no longer virgins by the time of marriage, this seems to be a rather orthodoxly pious belief that Muggleton could not shake going into his adult life.

Similarly interesting is the way that Muggleton treats his daughter, Sarah. Whilst describing his

---

[25] Alice Brabcová, *Marriage in Seventeenth-Century England: The Woman's Story* (University of West Bohemia, Plzeň, 2006) p.23.

marriages, he gives a glowing review of his daughter as 'the most experimental and knowing'st Women in Spiritual Things of that Sex in London'.[26] While contemporaries like John Evelyn were outspoken in praise for their daughters, Muggleton's words ring differently due to the spiritual parameter set by them.[27] Reeves' revelation goes as far as to name Sarah as 'the teacher of all the women of London.', although notably this is only women and does not suggest that Sarah was teaching men, rather that she, similarly to the Quakers, would teach a separate group. This inequality in representation is further

---

[26] Muggleton, 'The acts of the Witnesses', p.37.
[27] John Evelyn, *The Diary of John Evelyn: With an Introduction and Notes*. Edited by Austin Dobson, vol. 3, (Cambridge University Press, 2015.) p.301.

compounded in a statement by Phyllis Mack where she states that there is not a 'single extended work by a woman.' in the Muggletonian archive showing a deep fissure in the equality of the upper echelons of Muggletonians.[28] Shortly after Reeve states this, Sarah Muggleton was the first woman 'blessed to eternity' by Reeve.[29] The following description of Sarah's remarkable debating skills and the fact that Reeve's revelation directly named Sarah explains why Muggleton is particularly focused upon Sarah and gives her far more lofty praise than his other daughters that are barely mentioned.

---

[28] Phyllis Mack, *Visionary Women Ecstatic Prophecy in Seventeenth- Century England.* (London, University of California press, 1992) p.75.
[29] Muggleton 'The acts of the Witnesses' p.53.

Praising the roles of women within the Muggletonian cause did not end with relatives, however. In the acts of witness, Muggleton discusses Robert Phare, Governor of Cork in Ireland, who converted from Quakerism to Muggletonianism as did his wife.[30] He describes her as 'the chief Champion in this Faith of all the Women in that Nation.', with very lofty praise for what any other gender complementarian religious sect at the time may have just dismissed as a necessary role for a wife to fulfil for her husband. Phare's wife, Elizabeth is a very interesting woman. She is the daughter of Sir Thomas Herbert, the former personal attendant to Charles the first.[31]

---

[30] Muggleton 'The acts of the Witnesses', p.98.
[31] W. H. Welply, "Colonel Robert PHAIRE, "Regicide."His Ancestry, History,

This context is why she is so important to the Muggletonians. A woman of such a high standing converting to and spreading the word of the Muggletonians is incredibly valuable to the group and as a higher class, educated woman, she was a boon to the sect.

Some of the most revealing documents when analysing Reeve and Muggleton's attitudes towards women comes in their letters to their followers. As Christopher Hill, William Lamont and Barry Reay all highlight, the Muggletonian doctrines are the product of the influence of Calvinist predestination.[32]

---

and Descendants." *Journal, Cork Historical And Archaeological Society, Volume 30*, (1925) p.20.
< http://pigott-gorrie.blogspot.com/2013/12/irish-phayre-phaire-fair-families.html>
[Last accessed 13/04/2022]
[32] Christopher Hill, William Lamont and Barry Reay, *The world of the Muggletonians* (Temple Smith, London, 1983) p.27.

This expresses itself in Muggleton's letter to Mrs Elizabeth Dickinson in 1658 in which he writes 'And that thou may be sure I doe declare you one of the blessed of the Lord to all Eternity', ensuring Mrs Dickinson's place as one of the pre-destined.[33] This seems to be a result of her unwavering belief in Muggleton and Reeve's cause above all else. This granting of predestination based on her piety is preceded by Muggleton comforting her with the tale of a woman with "the bloody issue" (a condition that caused a woman to bleed from her genitals constantly and thus be deemed unclean by society) that was healed and salvaged, much as he

---

[33] Lodowick Muggleton 'Lodowick Muggleton to Elizabeth Dickinson, 1658. ' in *The Acts of the Witnesses : The Autobiography of Lodowick Muggleton and Other Early Muggletonian Writings*, ed. by T. L. Underwood, (Oxford University Press, Incorporated, 2000.) p.197.

professes himself and Reeve capable of. The significance of this attention to women and women's issues is that Calvinism tended to be patriarchal and gender complementarian in nature, treating women as appendages of men and subservient.[34] All of this shows that through spiritual means, Muggletonianism allowed the women of the group to gain the agency that they would not be afforded in other aspects of their lives or from other sects, even allowing them to directly contact the head of the sect and engage in open discussion with him.

---

[34]Steven Sandage et al. "Calvinism, Gender Ideology, and Relational Spirituality: An Empirical Investigation of Worldview Differences." *Journal of Psychology and Theology*, vol. 45, no. 1, (Mar. 2017) p.19.

In fact, Muggleton extends this same courteously to Elizabeth Dickinson Junior in a letter c.1674 in which he provides a sickly, dying young Muggletonian girl with the promise of predestination and happiness in the next life.[35] This interaction further highlights that it is not the gender of an individual Muggleton cares for, but rather merely their faith in himself and Reeve's beliefs. As she is the daughter of the aforementioned Elizabeth Dickinson, this faith would have been secured from a very early age, explaining Muggleton's disposition towards her. In the same year, Muggleton writes to Mrs Hampson

---

[35] Lodowick Muggleton 'Lodowick Muggleton to Elizabeth Dickinson, Jun.[ior], 6 March 1674/5. ' in *The Acts of the Witnesses : The Autobiography of Lodowick Muggleton and Other Early Muggletonian Writings*, ed. by T. L. Underwood, (Oxford University Press, Incorporated, 2000.) p.209.

of Cambridge who has recently lost her child whom she believed to be bewitched.[36] Instead of condemning Mrs Hampson's child as bewitched, Muggleton removed witchcraft as an option for blame and remarked that men women and children can all be afflicted, instead of blaming the child's death on a congenital illness. In the process, Muggleton relays a story of him and his second wife losing their child due to her dropsical nature (a term for a congenital illness that causes swelling, often leading to death), in this he merely regards this as an act of nature rather than blaming his wife. This willingness to empathise with women and

---

[36] Lodowick Muggleton 'Lodowick Muggleton to Mrs. Hampson of Cambridge, 11 June 1674.' in *The Acts of the Witnesses : The Autobiography of Lodowick Muggleton and Other Early Muggletonian Writings*, ed. by T. L. Underwood, (Oxford University Press, Incorporated, 2000.) pp.210-211.

their issues, especially when the social conduct of the time would have far more easily allowed for the blaming of the woman shows an ingrained gender-egalitarian view of the world that Muggleton seems to embody.[37]

Another interesting aspect of the Muggletonian worldview that relates to women is Muggleton's views on abortion. This comes from a passage in his writing *A True Interpretation Of The Witches of Endor* in which he discusses the idea of the quickening of children in the womb. Carla Spivack, a professor of law, has analysed quickening and abortion laws in the early modern period and

---

[37]Bruce Ware, *Summaries of the Egalitarian and Complementarian Positions.*(2007)
 <https://cbmw.org/2007/06/26/summaries-of-the-egalitarian-and-complementarian-positions/>
[Last accessed 17/02/2022]

established that while the abortion of pre-quickened children was not widely prosecuted or heavily condemned, it was still a taboo thing to highlight.[38] Therefore, Muggleton's religious justification and support for a still rather contentious form of reproductive rights. This is especially shown by the language that Muggleton used to describe the aborted child, not as such but rather states with regards to the process that 'the child, was not quick it was an insensible life, no more capable of pain than there is in death or a dead lump of the earth'.[39] Patricia Crawford and Laura Gowing use the 1672

---

[38] Carla Spivack "To "Bring Down the Flowers": The Cultural Context of Abortion Law in Early Modern England" *Wm. & Mary J. Women & The Law*, Volume 14. (2007) p.116.
[39] Lodowick Muggleton *A True interpretation of the Witches Of Endor* (1669, 1831 edition) p.29.
<http://www.muggletonian.org.uk/Early%20Muggletonian/Endor.htm> [Last Accessed 23/02/2022]

example of Mary Smith to discuss abortion and infanticide. In this case, Mary smith stands trial, accused of infanticide for merely being found alongside a dead child that she claims was miscarried in a fall.[40] This legal standpoint of guilty until innocent runs contrary to Muggleton's view that unless provably quickened at the time of abortion, the woman is innocent. This, tied with the passage's general theme of disregarding something as alive until it has quickened very much mirrors views that many would even find progressive today. Indeed, much of the modern pro-choice movement is tied up with the feminist movements of the last seventy years. This makes the brazen and

---

[40] Patricia Crawford and Laura Gowing. *Women's Worlds in Seventeenth-Century England.* (Routledge, 2000.) pp.25-26.

open support for these rights three hundred years before their modern mainstreaming rather shocking and a bold example of a primordial form of the modern reproductive rights movement, even more shockingly spearheaded by a heavily religious man from a time where patriarchy was extremely dominant.

In his writing *The Neck of the Quaker's Broken*, Muggleton debates with the Quakers along with a multitude of theological lines, one important aspect arises rather quickly, that of the 'reprobate angel'.[41] What is interesting is Muggleton's distinctions between the two "seeds" of humanity one of the

---
[41] Lodowick Muggleton, *The Neck of The Quakers Broken* (1663, 1756 edition) p.6.
<http://www.muggletonian.org.uk/Early%20Muggletonian/content%20files/Quaker%20broken.pdf>
[Last Accessed 24/02/2022]

serpent and one of Adam. As Elizabeth Hodgson has pointed out, Eve and her eating of the forbidden fruit has been a longstanding tool for religious men to illustrate and articulate their misogyny, yet the early 17th century marks a turning point in this tradition.[42] A reimagining of Eve began to take place to create a far more sympathetic view of Eve from many female authors. What stands out about Muggleton then is his defence of Eve with his role as the head of a male-lead radical religious sect. He argues that not only is Eve a sympathetic figure but that the seed of the serpent is, in fact, 'always in Opposition unto the Seed of the Woman, which is

---

[42]Elizabeth Hodgson,. "A 'Paraditian Creature': Eve and Her Unsuspecting Garden in Seventeenth-Century Literature." *Biblical Women in Early Modern Literary Culture, 1550–1700: 1550–1700*, edited by Victoria Brownlee And Laura Gallagher, (Manchester University Press, 2015) p.1.

the Seed of Adam, which is the Seed of Faith'[43]. With this, Muggleton not only defends Eve but places her alongside Adam in opposition to the corruption of the Devil himself.

This radical realignment of the view of Eve as not only the individual who is no longer responsible for the 'original sin' but is a force that opposes sin is a very radically feminist stance for its time. He then further elaborates on this point with scripture, using God's statement that 'The seed of the woman shall break the serpents head'[44] and highlighting that the apostles communicated their beliefs to both men and women (but not children) in order to further

---

[43] Lodowick Muggleton *The Neck of The Quakers Broken* (1663, 1756 edition) p.6. <http://www.mugbletonian.org.uk/Early%20Muggletonian/content%20files/Quaker%20broken.pdf> [Last Accessed 24/02/2022]

[44] Lodowick Muggleton *The Neck of The Quakers Broken* pp.92-93.

demonstrate his commitment to the belief that Eve and therefore women are not responsible for the original sin and therefore should be treated equally, just as the apostles did before them. Whilst the last portion has focussed on Muggleton's view of Eve, it is important to note that in Reeve's *A Transcendent Spiritual Treatise* he showed many of the same views that Muggleton would go on to hold. In this, Eve is further exonerated of her wrongdoing when Reeves wrote of Cain being the evil one and even declared Eve outrightly innocent in a clear double play in both the moral and legal sense.[45]

---

[45] John Reeve and Lodowick Muggleton 'A Transcendent Spiritual Treatises' in in *The Acts of the Witnesses : The Autobiography of Lodowick Muggleton and Other Early Muggletonian Writings*, ed. by T. L. Underwood, (Oxford University Press, Incorporated, 2000.) p.152.

Going even further than Muggleton however, he directly challenged the word of the bible, essentially declaring that the quote "the woman was deceived, and not the man." was no longer canonically accurate due to the revelations that he had received. This change rewrites millennia of history portraying Eve as the perpetrator of the original sin and instead places the blame on the serpent enticing her and then declaring Cain as evil above her. This notion goes way beyond the rewriting of the narrative on Eve as Muggleton would go on to do, but rather rewrites and amends biblical scripture in order to restore the image of a woman that for a long stretch of history was the main target for misogyny in the church. While, as

Christopher Hill pointed out, the Muggletonians were indeed a small group of hundreds, this break from the entire traditional history of the written bible as well as Muggleton's continued defence of this stance against the Quakers shows just how rigid these men were in defence of a feminist view of the mother of mankind. [46]

The equality-aimed standards set by Muggleton and Reeve, two men living in a patriarchal world, were enshrined by them in their founding documents and remained as key principles of the group throughout their lives. They spoke out for pre-quickening abortion, a taboo topic to this day. They elevated and promoted women as key guiding figures in

---
[46] Hill, Lamont and Reay, *The world of the Muggletonians*, p.55.

their sect as role models for other women, therefore further promoting their more liberal views to contemporary women who were often locked into gender complementarian religious views like that of Calvinism and offering a path towards an early, albeit rather tame by today's standards, form of female agency. By far, however, their most important contribution to the world of female liberation was that of the reimagining of Eve and the removal of the burden of the original sin from women. The amending of the Bible to do this is such a wildly radical yet surprisingly overlooked aspect of Muggletonian doctrine and the fact that Muggleton would spend the rest of his life defending these views shows a genuine commitment to the rehabilitation of the attitudes towards women. All of this combines to create an image of a sect that prizes its, for the time, liberal views on women and actively works towards their agency by providing a strong spiritual bedrock for it to stand upon.

Chapter 2: Muggletonian Community.

Community is a more explored area of Muggletonian life than the role of women is. Christopher Hill remarks that the Muggletonian community was the most 'informal sect of the seventeenth century.'[47] Despite this labelling, the Muggletonian fostered a rather present sense of community in both their lower and higher ranks. One way of doing this was through music. During the period of the civil wars, songs and ballads were key cultural touchstones for many groups. Angela Mcshane highlights that they were about the price of a loaf of bread and often disseminated for free in

---

[47] Christopher Hill, William Lamont and Barry Reay, *The world of the Muggletonians* (Temple Smith, London, 1983) p.35.

taverns, markets or on the side of homes.[48] Their popularity grew with the print trade and the easy, efficient, and cheap production of these materials allowed for their quick dissemination amongst communities.[49] In his wonderful book, Christopher marsh highlights that music held a key role in maintaining moral order through the 17th century idea that, due to its heavenly sound, music could only come from a good man.[50] This explains the prevalence of Muggletonian balladry as it further

---

[48] Angela McShane, "Drink, song and popular politics." *Popular Music, Volume 35* (2016) p.166.
[49] , Sarah Page Wisdom, *Ballads, Culture and Performance in England 1640-1660.* (Georgia State University, 2011.) p.18 <https://scholarworks.gsu.edu/cgi/viewcontent.cgi?article=1050&context=history_theses>
[Last accessed 10/03/22]
[50] Christopher Marsh, *Music and Society in Early Modern England,* (Cambridge, 2010) pp.59-64.

aids in creating a holy image of the founders through the notions of the time.

In the Muggletonian context, the first example we will look at comes from Nathaniel Powell. Whilst not one of the founding duo of Muggletonianism, Powell is still a significant figure in the group. Powell is responsible for writing *A true account of the trial and sufferings of Lodowick Muggleton* shortly after his trial in 1676. In which he is described as an eyewitness to Muggleton's trial.[51] In this he discusses Muggleton and his punishment, the whole time referring to him as his 'Lord'.[52] The

---

[51] Nathaniel Powell, *A True Account of the Trial and Suffering of Lodowick* (1808 edition)
<http://www.muggletonian.org.uk/Early%20Muggletonian/A%20True%20Account%20of%20the%20Trial.htm>
[Last accessed 12/03/22]
[52] Powell, *A True Account of the Trial and Suffering of Lodowick* p.20.

fact that his recounting goes on to be the official, published source for the trial from the Muggletonians' point of view shows his significance within the group and therefore verifies him as someone worthy of writing a ballad about the sect.

His song starts as a simplified recounting of the revelations that Reeve received, written in easily remembered rhymes:

'Hark hark I hear the Almighty's voice

Saying John Reeve I have made choice

Of thee my Messenger to be

To publish Secrets hid from thee.'[53]

---
[53] Nathaniel Powell, 'Song by Nathaniel Powell' in *The Acts of the Witnesses : The Autobiography of Lodowick Muggleton and Other Early Muggletonian Writings*,

The first half of the song is written from the point of view of the Lord, explaining to Reeve the Lord's choice to pick him before transitioning into a far longer piece on the devil and the consequences of not following the Lord.[54]

Where the song becomes interesting is in the latter verses when Powell begins to discuss the Mugbletonian "flock". In these verses, Powell details the fact that any followers of Muggletonianism are the chosen, predestined ones of society.[55] This being in song form would have been a great unifying point for the Muggletonian community. This ensures that these were sung

---

ed. by T. L. Underwood, (Oxford University Press, Incorporated, 2000.) p.215.
[54] Powell, 'Song by Nathaniel Powell' p.217.
[55] Powell, 'Song by Nathaniel Powell' p.215.

together or to the group, allowing for communal bonding over the fact that they were the chosen. Combining this with another one of the later verses that detail the fact that non-believers were doomed to burn in hell with the devil creates an atmosphere of self-congratulation amongst the 'chosen ones' of the world, bonding them in collective damnation of outsiders and perceived others. The end of Powell's song is rather revealing as well. It advocates for the praising of Reeve and Muggleton and declares them to be saints due to their willingness to accept the Lord's instructions and follow his words precisely.[56] Puritan doctrine believed in the idea of the "visible saint" in their society. This was the

---

[56] Powell, 'Song by Nathaniel Powell' p.216.

notion that saints were observable and identifiable through their actions and the way that they carried themselves, signs that most puritans were taught to spot in the church.[57] Given the fact that many key Muggletonians, including Reeve himself, moved around between radical groups and sects, it is not unlikely that Powell picked up this notion from the puritans and transferred it to Reeves and Muggleton.

This aids in creating an image of the Muggletonian community as a melting pot of radical religious ideas focused around the cult of personality of the two founders of the religion. While through modern

---

[57] Edmund S. Morgan *Visible saints, the history of a Puritan idea.* (New York university press, 1963) p.133.

<https://babel.hathitrust.org/cgi/pt?id=mdp.39015002599143&view=1up&seq=133&q1=saint> [Last accessed 15/03/2022]

eyes, this may seem like troubling behaviour, it was not necessarily uncommon for groups at the time. The lead Quaker George Fox, for example, was regarded as the key figure for their group alongside William Penn who was ultimately shunned in favour of pro-Fox leadership.[58] Clearly then, this leader worship was not unique on its own, but where Powell seems to exceed the praise that Fox received is in that designation of sainthood. The fact that this was done in song form would have helped to create further unity amongst two unchallengeable figures within the Muggletonian communities that aided to avoid the factionalism

---

[58] Melvin Endy. "George Fox and William Penn: Their Relationship and Their Roles within the Quaker Movement." *Quaker History*, vol. 93, no. 1, (2004) p.1.

that corrupted Quakerism with Penn's fall from grace.

In his untitled song, William Wood seems to go even further with the praise for Muggleton and Reeves. Wood is most recognizable in the modern eye as the man who painted the most recognisable portrait of Lodowick Muggleton. Similar to Powell, this delegation of such an important responsibility as to preserve a prophet's likeness in paint to William Wood shows his importance within the community and therefore explains his credentials when writing a song to be spread. In the seventh to eleventh stanzas of his work, Wood paints an image with words as striking as he does with his brush, that being a portrait of a strong, bold, enigmatic man when describing the men at the heart of his community.

Figure 1: Lodowicke Muggleton, by William Wood, circa 1674.

The eighth stanza is particularly illuminating when it comes to showing how these men were viewed. It begins with a proclamation that these men and their words are undefeatable and unchallengeable in terms of their position or, as Wood describes it: 'No Champions like these in this region doth dwelle'.[59] This aforementioned region remains ambiguous but could very well mean England as a whole as Wood was stationed at Braintree, ruling out the likelihood of London. This is key as it helps to build the image of a community very much aware of the atmosphere they exist in, an idea that will be picked up when viewing how the Muggletonians fit into their generation. What is key about this when analysing their communal behaviour, however, is this defensive stance against those others who

---

[59]William Wood, 'Song by William Wood' in *The Acts of the Witnesses : The Autobiography of Lodowick Muggleton and Other Early Muggletonian Writings*, ed. by T. L. Underwood, (Oxford University Press, Oxford, 2000) p.218.

claim to be the truest among them. Usually, for the Muggletonians, this was the Quakers. Douglas Greene remarked that they had 'One of the most bitter pamphlet wars of the later seventeenth century'[60].

The language of this song very well could have served as a public weapon in the war for religious validity between the two or as a bonding tool for the community in the face of an enemy of gargantuan proportions compared to their size. This politicisation of songs has its origins earlier in the century during the civil war when, as McShane points out, each side of the conflict began to

---

[60]Douglas Greene. "Muggletonians and Quakers: A Study in the Interaction of Seventeenth-Century Dissent." *Albion: A Quarterly Journal Concerned with British Studies*, vol. 15, no. 2, (1983) p.1.

increasingly politicise songs, as we see on a micro-scale with the Muggletonians and Quakers.[61] This reinforcing of the belief of superiority is carried into the next stanza in which Wood details the fact that these men have the same divine 'balm' that Jesus had, that being the ability to calm and heal the ill and dying. This impact giving of biblical powers to these men is once again amplified by the fact that these songs could have been used as public announcements of the community's key figures and a rallying cry for the divinity of these men. The final two stanzas are a continuation of this. The song ends with the statement that the men at the core of the community will finish God's 'mystery'.

---

[61]McShane, "Drink, song and popular politics."p.173

This is a final rallying statement that this group and these men are those who have been chosen by God, not any other individual or group and that they are indeed part of the godliest community.

Geographical regionality and the spread of its members are key for any religious community and the Muggletonians were no stranger to this. Despite its catholic reputation, Ireland appears to have been a key area for the Muggletonian cause. Cork seems to have been the epicentre of the Muggletonian's Irish congregation. Two sources show this. The first is a passage in Muggleton's *The acts of the Witnesses* mentioned in the previous chapter. This Focuses on Probert Phare or Phayre as it is commonly spelt. Phayre was, at the time, an extremely notable figure to convert to Muggletonianism. While Lamont, Reay and Hill mentioned Ireland and Phayre in *The World of The Muggletonians*, it is only in two small passages, the largest of which merely details that the Muggletonians made inroads to Ireland through the New Model Army.[62] This is being expanded upon by looking at Phayre as well as how the print movement allowed for the movement of documents into Ireland. Phayre's most infamous act was his presence at the drafting of the regicidal documents for which he was imprisoned in 1660 during the Restoration.[63]

---

[62] Christopher Hill, William Lamont and Barry Reay, *The world of the Muggletonians* (Temple Smith, London, 1983) p.56

According to Muggleton's writing, Phayre would become a beacon for conversion to Muggletonianism, with him listing all the reputable individuals that Phayre had converted.[64] These people are connected by a certain middle-class lifestyle, with two being military men, one a doctor and two merchants, showing a diverse range of professions that Muggletonians touched, even within a class bubble. In fitting with Muggletonian sources of communal pride, Phayre was formerly associated with the Quakers, a point that Muggleton was happy to emphasise in his description of the man. One of the people that

---

[63] Stephen Leslie. *Dictionary of national biography vol 45.* (New York Macmillan 1895-1900) pp.142-143
[64] Lodowick Muggleton 'The acts of the Witnesses' in *The Acts of the Witnesses : The Autobiography of Lodowick Muggleton and Other Early Muggletonian Writings*, ed. by T. L. Underwood, (Oxford University Press, Oxford, 2000.) p.98

Muggleton lists as a successful Irish convert was a merchant, George Gamble. Gamble is significant as we have a letter, addressed to him from one Alexander Delamain. Delamain bucks the trend of most Muggletonians, as Kate Peters points out, by actively aiding the Quakers in their publishing efforts.[65] What is most important about this, however, is the fact that Delamain is a notable Muggletonian within the highly influential radical book trade. This is key as it provides a window into how the Muggletonian community spread across England and Ireland. The content and recipient of this letter reveal how this was done in Cork.

---

[65] Kate Peters. *Print culture and the early Quakers* (Cambridge press, 2004) p.47

The letter details the dissemination of Thomas Powell's account of Muggleton's trial through Gamble, a noted merchant. This then shows the system for the spreading of the Muggletonian community into Ireland: an account of a key event or publication would be released through a book distributor like Delamain, then would be sent through to merchants like Gamble who would then sell these to either inform current Muggletonians or to preach to new ones in hope of attracting them into the sect. Even the limited understanding that Delamain imparts upon the field is extremely useful in looking at how the Muggletonian communities spread to typically religiously intolerant lands like Ireland at this time. Where analysing *The acts of the Witnesses* and the correspondence between Delamain and Gamble expands on this is by providing a direct link to the Irish expansion of the Muggletonians and the ever-expanding radical print network that span out of London and across the British Isles that Gamble was, as previously mentioned, entwined with through both the Muggletonians and the Quakers. This same network may explain why, like Lamont, Reay and Hill discussed when detailing their presence in Ireland, their smaller presence in Scotland.

Delamain is a wonderful window into the communal life of the Muggletonians. Clearly a close ally of Muggleton and useful due to his relatively decent social standing, Delamain appears numerous times in the records of the Muggletonians, most notably as a collector of Muggletonian documents and the author of the 'Great book' of the Muggletonians.[66] Clearly a focal point of the community, one important document shines a light upon a more obscure aspect of Muggletonian communal life. This is an expense sheet for a Muggletonian banquet. What is interesting about this dinner is not only the guestlist, containing the Delamain family but also what the group paid for and how much they paid. Around twenty people attended, many of which

---

[66] Hill, Lamont and Reay, *The world of the Muggletonians*, p.147

have been lost to history, but we do know Mr Delamain and his family attended, with a combined budget of four and three-quarter pounds.[67]

What is so telling about this is that the Bank of England's inflation calculator puts that figure in 2021 at a value of just over a thousand pounds, equating to each attendee paying around 60 pounds each for the event.[68] What this reveals about the Muggletonian community is that the higher ranking events required a relative amount of wealth to attend and shifts the communal feeling towards that of a middling-sorts social club featuring merchants

---

[67] Anon 'Expense Record, Dinner' in *The Acts of the Witnesses : The Autobiography of Lodowick Muggleton and Other Early Muggletonian Writings*, ed. by T. L. Underwood, (Oxford University Press, Oxford, 2000.) p.227
[68] <https://www.bankofengland.co.uk/monetary-policy/inflation/inflation-calculator>
[Last accessed 22/03/2022]

like Delamain. This is emphasised when looking at the expenses made by the group. The most telling of these is the paying of servants for the event, at only 2 shillings between them for the entire thing despite the sheer size of the meal.[69] This further reinforces the idea of the upper echelons of the Mugbletonian community being firmly entrenched in the middle class, as does the quarter of the budget spent on wine for the day, around £200 in modern terms. The wine could be explained as a social lubricant, helping in bonding the upper echelons of the sect. The list of luxury items that the party uses creates a contrast to the Puritans and their stricter views. This may link to the context of

---

[69] Anon 'Expense Record, Dinner' p.228

the period of the dinner in 1682 and the Stuart restoration beforehand. Micheal Winship discusses the fact that puritanism had moved to a more moderate, less conformist view in the aftermath of the Restoration.[70] This, combined with the generally more open attitudes of the restoration period may have led to an uptick in the middle-class representation in the Muggletonian community.

Returning to Delamain, his fellow copier of the Muggletonian documents, Tobiah Terry provides one last interesting document when looking at the Muggletonian community. Rather uniquely, this

---

[70] Michael Winship,. "Defining Puritanism In Restoration England: Richard Baxter And Others Respond To 'A Friendly Debate.'" *The Historical Journal*, vol. 54, no. 3, (Cambridge University Press, 2011.)p.714

document is an acrostic poem.[71] As Junho Cho of Stellenbosch University highlights in his work on Biblical acrostic poetry, choosing the form of the poem says just as much about the poem as its content does.[72] In this case, we can rather safely assume that Terry was aiming to emulate this very same religious poetry with his own acrostic. This, combined with Terry's role as a copier shows that he was a fairly well educated and learned man for the time to be able to interpret both biblical and radical texts to such a degree and then create a

---

[71] Tobiah Terry 'An Acrostic by Tobit [Tobiah] Terry.' in *The Acts of the Witnesses : The Autobiography of Lodowick Muggleton and Other Early Muggletonian Writings*, ed. by T. L. Underwood, (Oxford University Press, Oxford, 2000.) pp.226-227

[72] Junho Choi. *Understanding The Literary structures Of Acrostic Psalms an Analysis Of Selected Poems* (Stellenbosch University, 2013) p.18 <https://www.academia.edu/40278322/UNDERSTANDING_THE_LITERARY_STRUCTURES_OF_ACROSTIC_PSALMS_AN_ANALYSIS_OF_SELECTED_POEMS> [Last accessed 22/03/2022]

hybrid of the two formats. This reveals that the Muggletonian community relied on a core of reasonably educated individuals like Terry and Delamain to create works to spread the words of the witnesses, as shown by the fact that Delamain had written his own song about the two. The words that the acrostic forms are, of course, the names of the two witnesses further emphasising their cult of personality within the group. The content of the poem is more of the same, praise for the witnesses and demonisation of any outside beliefs that contradict them.

All of this works to solidify the idea that rather than the ordinary priests of a religious order that the

Muggletonians lack, as Lamont, Reay and Hill highlighted when discussing the informality of the sect, the Muggletonians clearly are more bound by an equally strong love of the witnesses and a shared demonisation of any outside of the order. The Muggletonians are a movement led by the middling sorts that wisely utilised the established radical religious print networks and distributors to gain a small but rabid community amongst the middling and lower orders of the British Isles to bolster the ranks of their sect.

Chapter 3: Muggletonians and their generation.

One final aspect to look at when considering the Muggletonians as a social entity is to examine to what extent the Muggletonians belonged to a specific generation. What is meant by this is to look at the generation that the founders of this sect were born into, how it affected them and how much are they outliers from the others in their generation?

These men were clearly born into a tumultuous time. As Muggleton would detail in *The acts of the Witnesses*, Reeve was born in 1608 in Wiltshire to a family in decline, with his father being a failing clerk to a deputy of Ireland. Muggleton was born in London to a blacksmith.[73] Reeve would move to London and work as a tailor alongside Muggleton as an apprentice. What is key about this is the economics of the tailoring trade at the time. In the early 1620s, the time at which the two men would have been starting their apprenticeships, English cloth had gone into decline in foreign markets. In addition to this, as Keith Wrightson highlights, agricultural production began to slow down as the population moved towards urbanisation, with over a quarter of England living in this environment by 1670.[74] The economic issues around this time got

---

[73] Lodowick Muggleton 'The acts of the Witnesses' in *The Acts of the Witnesses : The Autobiography of Lodowick Muggleton and Other Early Muggletonian Writings*, ed. by T. L. Underwood, (Oxford University Press, Oxford, 2000.) p. 31.
[74] Keith Wrightson, *Earthly Necessities*, (Penguin, London, 2002) p.172.

so bad that the privy council called a commission to investigate this.[75]

What this tells us is that Reeve and Muggleton were relatively low-born men raised in a failing industry. These men would have been part of a whole generation raised in economic uncertainty and failing job prospects. As history shows, many individuals born into these economic conditions, especially with Charles I's move towards authoritarian personal rule in the late 1620s, are far more susceptible to radicalism. The Russian Revolution of the early 20th is a fine modern example of monarchical authoritarianism and

---

[75] Braxton Hall, *Creating Economy: Merchants in Seventeenth-Century England* (Thesis: George State University, 2017) p.28.

economic downturn breeding radicalism in a nation.

It is to this backdrop of radicalism that one key factor in shaping this generation's religious mindset comes to the fore, that being the rise of the Puritans. Muggleton details puritans visiting him in his youth as an apprentice in which he became enamoured with their knowledge of the Bible and their piety.[76] This encounter clearly had an impact on the young Muggleton. Kenneth Fincham and Peter Lake highlight the prevalence of the puritans as a popular force to be used to voice their opposition to Laudianism and the acts of the King without directly opposing him. [77] This use of

---

[76] Muggleton 'The acts of the Witnesses' P.32.

puritanism and anti-Laudianism as a form of pious radicalism fits with Alexandra Walsham's theory of sectarianism and religious decent as a generational feature for defining oneself and emphasising one's piousness that was mentioned in the introduction to this dissertation.[78]

Clearly then, the religious radicalism of this generation is an equally political and religious act. This is key as it places these men into a world where this behaviour is the norm and why, even when Reeves' vision occurred during the Protectorate, the men were ready to rebel. This was simply what their generation viewed as the norm,

---

[77] Peter Lake, Kenneth Fincham, 'Popularity, Prelacy and Puritanism in the 1630s: Joseph Hall Explains Himself', *The English Historical Review*, 443 (1996) p.871.
[78] Alexandra Walsham, "The Reformation Of The Generations: Youth, Age And Religious Change In England, c. 1500–1700." *Transactions of the Royal Historical Society*, (vol. 21, 2011) p.114.

to rebel against the orthodoxy, no matter who it was that held power at the time. While Walsham highlights that many protestant generations before Muggleton and Reeve were rebellious, what is so distinctive about their rebellion is their direct link to the Lord himself.[79] While George Fox of the Quakers similarly believed that he had received a revelation, what propelled Reeve and Muggleton above this is their continued and staunch reliance on their singular revelation and role of prophets of the lord to create a uniquely structured sect with such heavy focus on the founders.[80]

---

[79] Walsham, "The Reformation Of The Generations: Youth, Age And Religious Change In England, c. 1500–1700." P.105.
[80] George Fox, *Journal of George Fox,* (1694) <https://web.archive.org/web/20070926224332/http://www.strecorsoc.org/gfox/ch01.html>
[Archived online on 26 september 2007, Last Accessed 24/02/2022]

One rebellious sect closely linked with the Muggletonians is that of the Ranters. In an article critiquing fellow historian J.C. Davis, Christopher Hill highlights the links between the Ranters, the Quakers and the Muggletonians when discussing how the latter two had to distance themselves from the former for fear of similar persecution to the Ranters.[81] The reason why this link is so key is twofold. Firstly, it shows a clear common ancestorial path between these three groups to form such similarly radical groups, further supporting the theory that the radicalism of this generation is genuinely both unique and generation-wide. Secondly, it shows a generational consciousness in

---
[81]Christopher Hill, 'The Lost Ranters? A Critique of J. C. Davis', *History Workshop*, 24 (1987) p.136.

those born in the first 30 years of the 17th century, influenced by the religious and social turmoil of the time, surrounding the notion of radicalism and the impact that the other groups around them were having. This is supported in *The acts of The Witnesses* where Muggleton details a meeting between himself, Reeve and two Ranters, Proudlove and Remington who had planned with three unfortunates to curse Muggleton and Reeve.[82]

This is very revealing as it shows a generation of not only communicating and intertwined radical groups. This is because, Proudlove, as David Como exposes, was a prolific man when attacking other sects. Weirdly enough, prior to attacking

---

[82] Muggleton 'The acts of the Witnesses' P.63.

Muggleton and Reeve, Proudlove had invaded the dreams of the Puritan minister Edward Howes.[83] This shows a hugely interconnected generation of radicals, being so prominent that they began to appear in others' dreams. While eccentric, this shows the generational consciousness that was previously discussed as it shows a large group of intertwined sects that were all formed within a generation that was all so aware of each other that they began to attack each other and even haunt each other's dreams. The question may arise as to whether this conflict is solely due to the fact that they shared a generation and age. This is difficult to

---

[83]David R. Como, *Blown by the Spirit: Puritanism and the Emergence of an Antinomian Underground in Pre-Civil-War England* (California: Stanford University Press, 2004) p.444.

answer. One solution may lie in the fact, that these groups only ever questioned each other and not the ideas of the generation previous, for example, Muggleton and Reeve are not noted as remarking on Laudianism, a key point of debate of the decades previous to their emergence. This may be because of their generation, or possibly, as Eichinger suggests, them being trapped in a radical bubble at the radical end of the religious spectrum.[84]

One image of the Muggletonian that holds weight is that of them being a generational endpoint for religious radicals. The evidence for this comes from those who were affiliated with the group. The

---

[84] Juleen Audrey Eichinger, 'The Muggletonians: A People Apart' (Dissertation: Western Michigan University, 1999) pp.21-24.

natural place to start is the key founder of the sect, John Reeve. Reeve was affiliated with the Ranter John Robins, a wonderful example of a key figure when looking at these groups' generational views. Robins is mentioned as a Ranter and a deceiver by Muggleton in his *The acts of the Witnesses*. Muggleton further associated him with John Tauny whom he describes as ahead of both the Ranters and Quakers.[85] This is key as this further corroborates previous points that the heads of these radical sects formed a network within their generation at the radical end of the political spectrum through Tauny who would have been connected to someone like Delamain who, as

---

[85] Muggleton 'The acts of the Witnesses' p.57.

previously stated, actively aided the Quakers alongside being a Muggletonian. Someone like Muggleton becomes a nexus of these radical forces and a touchstone for the generation. Thus, the Muggleotanians were arguably the sect least prone to the radicalism of someone like John Robins. In fact, many like Reeve who flirted with these individuals gravitated towards Muggletonianism and became far less radical than the Ranters as evidenced by the fact that the Ranters faced legislative backlash and the Muggletonians did not. The same is true of individuals like Lawrence Clarkson, as mentioned in the introduction.

One of the most telling aspects of the primary sources is the reaction of the founders to the other radical leaders in their generation. One example of this is John Tannye. Also, in *The acts of the Witnesses*, John Tannye is described by Muggleton as a man who wished to gather the Jews of the world and lead them to Jerusalem.[86] Yet this was not the first time Tannye was mentioned. As early as 1656, Muggleton and Reeve wrote in *A Divine Looking Glass* a denouncement of Tannye proclaiming him as a 'counterfeit high priest' for the Jewish people.[87] This tells us that Muggleton and Reeve's perceptions of their radical generation

---

[86] Muggleton 'The acts of the Witnesses', p.40.
[87] Lodowick Muggleton, John Reeve, *A Divine Looking-Glass* (London: Catchpool and Trent, 1846) p. 143.

stretched outside of the Protestant or even Christian world. The fact that the men were aware of a self-proclaimed Jewish leader, that Muggleton even went as far as to mention the circumcising of, so shortly after the re-admittance of the Jews into England shows just how much of a web of radicals there was in this generation of individuals. Furthermore, the existence of a radical, self-proclaimed, Jewish leader in England at the time shows just how radical of a generation there was.

If one is to consider Walsham's theory of generation radicalism by removing oneself from the orthodoxy, again alongside the context of the age, the appearance of a Jewish leader makes sense.

This is not a mere bucking of the orthodoxy of the puritan head of England by offering a separate branch of Protestantism, this was offering a completely separate religious ideology as a radical alternative. If the former is seen as piety, the latter would have had Tannye considering himself a prophet, as is proven by Muggleton and Reeve's decrying of the man. This reaction to Tannye also further supports the idea that, while radical, the Muggletonians crafted a niche as a reactionary force against the ultra-radical, as shown by their reaction to John Robins.

One other group that the Muggletonians had a harsh reaction to was the Quakers. By this point, it is no surprise that the Quakers would reappear but their role in forming the Muggletonian view of their generation cannot be understated. One example of this is Muggleton's ongoing feud with the Quaker leader William Penn. One interesting criticism of Penn is that Penn's father was a man of 'estate'.[88] Where this ties into the idea of the generational consciousness and links back to the start of this chapter. Muggleton defined himself and Reeve as working-class men from poor backgrounds, growing up in an economic downturn that would have affected their whole generation. This economic background, however, did not bond as much as the generational link as it created a

---

[88] Lodowick Muggleton, *An Answer to William Penn, Quaker,* pp.128-129. (London, 1835) pp.128-129.

bond that Muggleton kept with the working class, even as he moved up into the middling sorts.

This, therefore, explains Muggleton's animosity towards Penn as he would not consider Penn part of this radical generation as he does not share the general experience of the rest of the generation due to his father's landed position. Muggleton may well have seen Penn as a beacon of the orthodox past, a privately educated reminder of the political elites that aided in the personal rule and long parliament, the very same force that Walsham claims these radicals counted themselves in opposition to. Furthermore, this explains why, despite the Quaker's relatively moderation, Muggleton held someone like Penn in such serious opposition. This is all supported by Muggleton's further criticism of Penn's father. Later in the aforementioned section, Muggleton accused Penn's father of being a war profiteer and therefore accused Penn of profiting from suffering that had devastated the rest of their generation. This further isolation from the generational consciousness helps to understand how Muggleton defines himself within it. Muggleton, therefore, sees himself as a lower-order champion of a war-torn generation, in touch with the people and championing their needs in such difficult times as opposed to using it to his advantage.

Muggleton continues his attack on Penn by attacking his theological roots. Muggleton plays upon his generation's Puritanism by highlighting that his spiritual guidance came purely from the bible.[89] He puts this in contrast with Penn and his University education. In particular, Muggleton attacks the fact that Penn learnt at university from History books and classics, focussing on the past, especially those of old religious texts, aligning him with outdated and disgraced religious views that anyone of their generation would have quickly dismissed.[90] This further supports the idea of Muggleton priding himself on his connection to the present and his generation as opposed to Penn, who

---

[89] Muggleton „*An Answer to William Penn, Quaker*, pp.121-122.
[90] Muggleton „*An Answer to William Penn, Quaker*, p.III.

is further painted as a relic of the past and a pretender, merely pretending to align with the radical values of the generation. The aforementioned focus on puritanism is also interesting when analysing Muggletons opposition to Penn. Muggleton highlights that he moved from Puritanism and became more humble when founding Muggletonianism.[91] He contrasts this with Penn's movement from Puritan, to Ranter and then to Quaker, calling him a double impostor for using both as a guise to fit into their generation. Muggleton's opposition to Penn in this regard may seem to break Walsham's theory but the fact that Muggleton uses the generational touchstone of the

---

[91] Muggleton ,*An Answer to William Penn, Quaker*, p.120.

puritanical mainstream and his connection to him then further elaborates that he went in a more radical yet humble direction, strengthening Walsham's theory further.

Overall, the ways that the Muggletonians fit within their generation are complex and myriad. They define themselves as subordinate heroes, opposing the corruption of the rich. They position themselves as the heroes of the war trodden against those who profited. They position themselves as radical zealots, stepping beyond the orthodoxy of the past, yet they also position themselves as bulwarks against ultra-radical groups and figures that may try to oppose them. Out of all of this, the image of the

Muggletonians becomes that as an essence of the desirable qualities of their generation; radical yet not too far, pious but not regressively orthodox and respectable without being elitist.

Conclusion.

This dissertation has provided a social history of the Muggletonians during the lifetime of Muggleton himself, assessing how they lived, what they believed and what brought them together. In doing so, it has attempted to go beyond the class-focussed Marxist history typical of Christopher Hill. This is significant as it ensures that the group is afforded a far rounder, fuller view as has been done with over groups like the Quakers and Ranters.

One heavily under-researched area of the Muggletonians that this dissertation has aimed to cover is that of women, both with regards to the founders' attitudes towards them and their roles in the group. The relatively large number of sources for the group that spoke directly about this is significant in showing just how central women, both contemporary and Biblical, were to the Muggletonians. The Muggletonian focus on the rehabilitation of the image of Eve and original sin is central to their views on women. When Reeve wrote this in *A Transcendent Spiritual Treatises* he proved the group's commitment to the promotion of women, even if it ran counter to centuries of religious orthodoxy. Their reliance on key women such as Muggleton's daughter shows the level that these men relied on women to be beacons and role models for the other women within their generation when it comes to joining the Muggletonian sect. However, ultimately these men were products of their time and Muggleton's traditional attitudes to marriage and virginity in women show this. Yet even with these attitudes, Muggleton still remains respectful to every woman that he mentions or is in direct contact with, except, of course, those connected with Quakerism at which point they are insulted equally and alongside their husbands.

The community of the Muggletonians was also explored in this dissertation. Whereas Hill's work has often boiled the Muggletonian's down to economic communities, this dissertation has shown the social glue that bonded the sect. One key way that they did this was through their songs. These were shown to be odes to the founders of the sect, glorifying them with recommendations for sainthood. This cult of personality allowed them to become an unquestionable point of unity within the group, allowing them to avoid the power struggles, leaderless anarchism and descent into factionalism that befell other groups like the Quakers and Ranters. These groups and the Muggletonian opposition to them also allowed for communal unity. By defining themselves by those they opposed, especially William Penn and the Quakers, it allowed for greater cohesion as an identifiable great, even when spread across the British Isles. This geographical spread in membership and the means by which it was achieved is also a novel addition to the academia on the Muggletonians. By looking at how these books were physically spread through merchants like Delamain, Hill's work on defining the Muggletonians as a group primarily containing members of the middling sort is directly tied into the reasons that they managed to achieve the range they did with such small numbers.

Finally, this dissertation explored the generation that this sect was formed and why this affected the group so much. This dissertation has shown that in a generation of radicals, Muggleton defined himself and Reeve firstly by their upbringing. This is shown in *The acts of the Witnesses* where

Muggleton describes their youth in terms of their economic status and trade. This is notable as he uses this previous to this writing to decry William Penn as a fraud of the radical generation, a university-educated, classically read son of a war profiteering landowner. How this differs from Hill's conclusions is that even as Muggleton shifted to become a member of the middling sorts, he kept these same opinions, showing that it was his view of Penn as an obstacle to generational progress and not economic that motivated Muggleton's dislike of him. Muggleton's vicious opposition to this lifestyle, alongside his opposition to the more radical sects in society at the time, shows that even within such a radical generation, Muggleton and

Reeve still had their limits and viewed themselves as the bulwarks of their generation against the ultra-radicalism, particularly of the Quakers and Ranters that they encountered. This is due to their generational default of relying upon a puritanical basis as the foundation for their radical beliefs and seeing a betrayal of this as an overstepping of the Muggletonians' self-imposed radical boundaries, as seen in *A divine Looking Glass*.

However, naturally, the story of the social history of the Muggletonians is far from complete. As social history grows more as an academic field and the historiography continues to move away and against the Marxist base of Hill, more will inevitably be written on these fascinating individuals. More can undoubtedly be written on the generational aspect of the Muggletonians as this field is so sparse when looking at the group. The greatest hope for this field would be another spontaneous discovery of a Muggletonian archive like the one in 1979 that allowed for the primary documents for this dissertation to be viewed. Ultimately, however, any future work in this field looking at these wonderfully eccentric individuals would require another lost sheep to find it.

Bibliography:

Images:

Lodowicke Muggleton, by William Wood, circa 1674

<https://en.wikipedia.org/wiki/File:Lodowicke_Muggleton_by_William_Wood.jpg>

[Last accessed 29/04/2022]

Primary Sources:

Anon 'Expense Record, Dinner' in *The Acts of the Witnesses : The Autobiography of Lodowick Muggleton and Other Early Muggletonian Writings*, ed. by T. L. Underwood, (Oxford University Press, Oxford, 2000.)

Clarkson, Lawrence, *The Lost Sheep Found*, (London: Printed for the author, 1660)

Evelyn, John, *The Diary of John Evelyn: With an Introduction and Notes*, ed. by Austin Dobson (Cambridge: Cambridge University Press, 2015)

Muggleton, Lodowick *A True interpretation of the Witches Of Endor* (1669, 1831 edition)<http://www.muggletonian.org.uk/Early%20Muggletonian/Endor.htm> [Last Accessed 23/02/2022]

Muggleton, Lodowick, *The Neck of The Quakers Broken* (1663, 1756 edition)

<http://www.muggletonian.org.uk/Early%20Muggletonian/content%20files/Quaker%20broken.pdf> [Last Accessed 24/02/2022]

Muggleton, Lodowick 'Lodowick Muggleton to Elizabeth Dickinson, 1658. ' in *The Acts of the Witnesses : The Autobiography of Lodowick Muggleton and Other Early Muggletonian Writings*, ed. by T. L. Underwood, (Oxford University Press, Incorporated, 2000.)

Muggleton, Lodowick, Reeve, John, *A Divine Looking-Glass* (London: Catchpool and Trent, 1846)

Muggleton, Lodowick'Lodowick Muggleton to Elizabeth Dickinson, Jun.[ior], 6 March 1674/5. ' in *The Acts of the Witnesses : The Autobiography of Lodowick Muggleton and Other Early Muggletonian Writings*, ed. by T. L. Underwood, (Oxford University Press, Incorporated, 2000.)

Muggleton, Lodowick'The acts of the Witnesses' in *The Acts of the Witnesses : The Autobiography of Lodowick Muggleton and Other Early Muggletonian Writings*, ed. by T. L. Underwood, (Oxford University Press, Oxford, 2000.)

Powell, Nathaniel, *A True Account of the Trial and Suffering of Lodowick* (1808 edition)

Powell, Nathaniel, 'Song by Nathaniel Powell' in *The Acts of the Witnesses : The Autobiography of Lodowick Muggleton and Other Early Muggletonian Writings*, ed. by T. L. Underwood, (Oxford University Press, Incorporated, 2000.)

Reeve, John and Lodowick Muggleton 'A Transcendent Spiritual Treatises' in in *The Acts of the Witnesses : The Autobiography of Lodowick Muggleton and Other Early Muggletonian Writings*, ed. by T.L. Underwood, (Oxford University Press, Incorporated, 2000.)

Terry, Tobiah 'An Acrostic by Tobit [Tobiah] Terry.' in *The Acts of the Witnesses : The Autobiography of Lodowick Muggleton and Other Early Muggletonian Writings*, ed. by T. L. Underwood, (Oxford University Press, Oxford, 2000.)

Wood, William. 'Song by William Wood' in *The Acts of the Witnesses : The Autobiography of Lodowick Muggleton and Other Early Muggletonian Writings*, ed. by T. L. Underwood, (Oxford University Press, Incorporated, 2000.)

Secondary Sources:

Brabcová, Alice, *Marriage in Seventeenth-Century England: The Woman's Story* (Plzeň: University of West Bohemia, 2006)

Bradstock, Andrew, *Radical Religion in Cromwell's England : A Concise History from the English Civil War to the End of the Commonwealth* (London: I. B. Tauris & Company, Limited, 2010)

Choi, Junho. *Understanding The Literary structures Of Acrostic Psalms an Analysis Of Selected Poems* (Stellenbosch University, 2013)

Como, David. R, *Blown by the Spirit: Puritanism and the Emergence of an Antinomian Underground in Pre-Civil-War England* (California: Stanford University Press, 2004)

Crabtree, Sarah A, Jankowski, Peter J, Schweer-Collins, Maria L, Sandage, Steven J, 'Calvinism, Gender Ideology, and Relational Spirituality: An Empirical Investigation of Worldview Differences', *Journal of Psychology and Theology*, 45, (2017)17 – 32

Crawford, Patricia, Gowing, Laura, *Women's Worlds in Seventeenth-Century England* (Oxford: Routledge, 2000)

Dow, F. D, *Radicalism in the English Revolution 1640-1660* (Oxford: Blackwell, 1985)

Eichinger, Juleen Audrey, *The Muggletonians: A People Apart* (Dissertation: West Michigan University, 1999)

Endy, Melvin. "George Fox and William Penn: Their Relationship and Their Roles within the Quaker Movement." *Quaker History*, vol. 93, no. 1, (Friends Historical Association, 2004)

Fincham, Kenneth, Lake, Peter, 'Popularity, Prelacy and Puritanism in the 1630s: Joseph Hall Explains Himself', *The English Historical Review*, 443 (1996) pp.856 – 871

Greene, Douglas. "Muggletonians and Quakers: A Study in the Interaction of Seventeenth-Century Dissent." *Albion: A Quarterly Journal Concerned with British Studies*, vol. 15, no. 2, (The North American Conference on British Studies, 1983)

Hall, Braxton, Creating Economy: Merchants in Seventeenth-Century England (Thesis: George State University, 2017)

Hill, Christopher, 'The Lost Ranters? A Critique of J. C. Davis', *History Workshop*, 24 (1987) pp.134 – 140

Hill, Christopher, 'The Muggletonians', *Past & Present*, 1 (1984) pp.153 – 159

Hill, Christopher, with William Lamont and Barry Reay, *The World of the Muggletonians* (Temple Smith, London, 1983)

Hill, Christopher, *The world turned upside down: Radical Ideas during the English Revolution* (Penguin Books, 2019 edition)

Hodgson, Elizabeth, 'A 'Paraditian Creature': Eve and Her Unsuspecting Garden in Seventeenth-Century Literature', *Biblical Women in Early Modern Literary Culture, 1550–1700: 1550–1700*, ed. by Victoria Brownlee and Laura Gallagher, (Manchester University Press, 2015)

Hutton, Ronald, *The British Republic 1649-1660* (Basingstoke: Macmillan, 2000)

Hughes, Ann, *Gender and the English Revolution* (London: Routledge, 2012)

Ingle, H. Larry, 'A Quaker Woman on Women's Roles: Mary Penington to Friends, 1678', *Journey of Women in Culture and Society*, 16 (1991) pp.587 – 589

Leslie, Stephen. *Dictionary of national biography vol 45.* (New York Macmillan 1895-1900)

Marsh, Christopher, *Music and Society in Early Modern England* (Cambridge: Cambridge, 2010)

Mack, Phyllis, *Visionary Women Ecstatic Prophecy in Seventeenth-Century England* (London: University of California press, 1992)

McShane, Angela, 'Drink, song and popular politics' *Polular Music,* 35 (2016) pp.166–190

Morgan, Edmund. *Visible saints, the history of a Puritan idea.* (New York university press, 1963)

Page, Sarah. Wisdom*, Ballads, Culture and Performance in England 1640-1660.* (Georgia State University, 2011.)

Peters, Kate. *Print culture and the early Quakers* (Cambridge: Cambridge press, 2004)

Raymond, Joad, *Seventeenth-Century Print Culture* (University of East Anglia, 2004)
<https://warwick.ac.uk/fac/arts/ren/researchcurrent/archive/newberry/collaborativeprogramme/ren-

earlymod-communities/britishandamericanhistories/summerworkshop/knights/raymond_on_print.pdf> [Last accessed 17/03/2022]

Richardson, R. C, *The Debate on the English Revolution* (Manchester: Manchester University Press, 1998)

Spivack, Carla, 'To "Bring Down the Flowers": The Cultural Context of Abortion Law in Early Modern England', *Wm. & Mary J. Women & The Law*, 14 (2007) pp.107 - 152

Ware, Bruce, *Summaries of the Egalitarian and Complementarian Positions*

<https://cbmw.org/2007/06/26/summaries-of-the-egalitarian-and-complementarian-positions/> [Last accessed 17/02/2022]

Thomas, Keith, 'Women And The Civil War Sects', *Past & Present*, 1 (1958) pp.42 – 62

Walsham, Alexandra, 'The Reformation Of The Generations: Youth, Age And Religious Change In England, c. 1500–1700' *Transactions of the Royal Historical Society*, 21 (2011) pp.93 – 121

Welply, W. H, "Colonel Robert PHAIRE, "Regicide."His Ancestry, History, and

Descendants." Journal, Cork Historical And Archaeological Society, Volume 30, (1925) <http://pigott-gorrie.blogspot.com/2013/12/irish-phayre-phaire-fair-families.html> [Last accessed 13/04/2022]

Winship, Michael. "Defining Puritanism In Restoration England: Richard Baxter And Others Respond To 'A Friendly Debate.'" *The Historical Journal*, vol. 54, no. 3, (Cambridge: Cambridge University Press, 2011.)

Wrightson, Keith. *Earthly Necessities* (London: Penguin, 2002)

Printed in Great Britain
by Amazon